5 Marketing Mistakes That Are Costing You Clients and Cash

DERRICK BANES

ISBN: 1517504996
ISBN-13: 978-1517504991

DEDICATION

I dedicate this book to my lovely wife and my kids, as they unknowingly motivate me to continually strive to leave a legacy behind that they can one day build upon.

CONTENTS

To receive **FREE** marketing tips, marketing product reviews, and monthly product discounts, visit <u>**www.24hrprinter.com**</u> and subscribe to our email list!

INTRODUCTION

If you search the phrase "what is marketing" on Google, the results will provide the action or business of promoting and selling products or services. To break it down even further, marketing is simply creating awareness that you exist. I wrote this book to help business owners and some of my very own clients understand the fundamentals of marketing and share valuable knowledge that I've learned over the years helping businesses grow.

Marketing is far more than a simple advertisement, webpage or flyer. It is about establishing yourself as an expert, attracting the clients that you want while avoiding catering towards those that may not be a good fit. Marketing entails presenting the right message to the right audience at the right time, to produce a desired set of results.

Marketing takes resources. Whether you're spending your own time or paying someone to do it for you, there is a cost associated to marketing. For the vast majority of business owners that I've come across, marketing is a necessity! Few have the luxury of running a business where clients will walk right through the front door on their own. If you're not consistently offering your products and services letting people know you exist, your business will eventually FAIL.

What can be confusing to business owners are the hundreds of products and methods of execution, but successful marketing strategies will differ from industry to industry and from company to company. What worked for company A, may not work for company B. Time and time again I've seen business owners make the same mistakes repeatedly. These mistakes don't just cause an inconvenience, they are costing you clients and cash!

-Derrick Banes

MISTAKE #1
YOUR MARKETING TO EVERYONE

"Everyone is NOT your customer." - Seth Godin

No matter how unique a skateboard company is, they probably won't make many sales at nursing homes. Position is the core of the definition of what marketing is. Marketing is putting the right product in the right place, at the right price, at the right time. If you are not positioning your services in the right place at the right time, you're wasting your efforts.

To know how to position your message, you need to define who your target customer truly is. A customer profile of your ideal client defines demographics as well as preferences, fears, motivations, and goals. It is the foundation that all of your marketing messages will be created around.

Say you are a personal trainer and your ideal clients are middle-age men that want to get back in shape. Your customer profile may look like this: Sam is 45 years old, has 3 kids and lives in the suburbs. He works 50 hours per week, sits at a desk all day and has a 20 minute commute. Since he works 10 hours a day and spends an hour commuting, he doesn't have much time to work out. Most likely, his only option is late at night after the kids are in bed. With this profile in mind, your marketing messages can appeal to someone who's sedentary lifestyle and busy schedule leaves them tired with little time to work out. You can target pain points like having limited time, or wanting more energy to play with their kids. Messaging about bodybuilding and workouts that take 2 hours a day are not going to peak this potential client's interest.

MARKETING MASTERY TIP #1

FOCUS YOUR MARKETING EFFORTS TOWARDS YOUR IDEAL CLIENT

Exercise: Identify Your Ideal Client

What type of clients do you like to work with?

_____

_____

_____

What challenges do your clients face?

_____

_____

_____

What are the benefits that your clients get from using your product or service?

_____

_____

_____

MISTAKE #2
NOT DIFFERENTIATING YOURSELF FROM YOUR COMPETITION

"You can't look at the competition and say you're going to do it better. You have to look at the competition and say you're going to do it differently." - Steve Jobs

Chances are there are other companies offering the same services as you. A unique selling proposition (USP) is what makes you and your business unique. What is it about you and your services that would make a potential client choose you over your competitors? What makes you unique? Why should people choose you? If you can't pinpoint why someone would choose you then you cannot target your marketing efforts properly. If your marketing isn't targeted, you might as well be throwing money out the window.

Even companies that have massive advertising budgets craft their marketing around their unique selling proposition. Carefully observe any popular company and you'll notice that their messaging always pushes their unique selling proposition.

- Walmart - "Save money. Live better."
- Tom's Shoes - "With every product you purchase, TOMS will help a person in need. One for One."
- Husky Tools - "Toughest name in tools." (Company offers a lifetime warranty)
- Energizer Batteries - "They keep going and going and going."

To find your USP, put yourself in your customer's shoes. Why do they use your service? There's often more to it than the core service that you offer. What solution do you provide for them? Why do people choose Target over Walmart? Both sell the same types of products at a discount; however, Target focuses on "affordable chic couture" products that attract style-conscious customers.

You need to know what motivates your customer's buying decisions. Are they looking for value or a unique style? Do they care about appearances, convenience or a specific expertise? Once you understand your customer and their motivations, you can craft your unique selling position.

MARKETING MASTERY TIP #2

Create a Unique Selling Proposition (USP)

Exercise: Create Your USP

What is it about you and/or your services that would make a potential client choose you over your competitors?

_____

_____

_____

What makes you unique?

_____

_____

_____

Why should people choose you?

_____

_____

_____

MISTAKE #3
SPENDING TOO MUCH TIME AND MONEY
ON OUTBOUND MARKETING

"If you have more money than brains, you should focus on outbound marketing. If you have more brains than money, focus on inbound marketing." - Guy Kawasaki

The most common outbound marketing strategies are radio, tv, and magazines. Before I go any further, let me point out I'm not saying outbound marketing is bad. It is a more conventional method where most small businesses do not have the resources or funding to properly leverage and track their cost of leads. With that being said, outbound marketing tends to be the most expensive and has the lowest rate of return.

Outbound marketing targets everyone in hopes of reaching those few who can actually use your products or services. This goes back to mistake #1 of not being able to identify your ideal customer. Big corporations can afford to spend thousands of dollars monthly on outbound marketing. However I have seen small business owners fail miserably by trying to mimic this approach, only to find themselves stressed from non-effective campaigns and a rapidly diminishing marketing budget.

This forces them to take on the task of marketing themselves, or attempt what I like to refer to as "band-aid marketing". The band-aid approach is when a business or entrepreneur knows they have to do something to generate business, but will try and cut every corner possible in the process. They will watch a quick online video and try several different strategies for a short amount of time. They may see a very slight peak in activity, but are never truly able to maximize the results of their marketing efforts strategy.

MARKETING MASTERY TIP #3

You don't have to have a big budget to get attention, but you do have to be interesting enough to keep the attention of your target audience.

Exercise: Measuring Your Marketing Effectiveness

What marketing strategies have you tried over the past 12 months?

_____

_____

_____

How did you gauge whether a marketing strategy is successful?

_____

_____

_____

What strategy aren't you using that you were using 6 months ago?

_____

_____

_____

MISTAKE #4
NOT LEVERAGING YOUR ONLINE PRESENCE

"Ignoring online marketing is like opening a business but not telling anyone." - Michael J. Schiemer

F ailing to leverage the power of the internet is one of the biggest marketing mistakes that a company can make. It doesn't matter how small your niche or how local your market is, you are missing clients if you don't have an online presence.

Gone are the days when you can write-off blogging, social media and e-mail marketing as fads. You need more than a simple website. You need a platform where you can establish yourself as an expert in your field and reach a wider audience. If you fail to leverage this platform, that leaves the door wide open for your competitors to reach the clients that were looking for you.

The first thing that a prospect will do is look online to see what others are saying about you. They are looking for information that shows you have some sort of credibility in your field. An updated blog and social media account along with mentions of your blog on third party websites gives strong social proof that you are an expert that will deliver the results that they are looking for.

Don't underestimate the power of an active presence on social media. Many companies that maintain a blog on their company website report that more than 50% of their business comes from their blog. An active online presence also provides an opportunity to build an e-mail list that allows you to instantly reach interested prospects. If you wanted to release a new service or offer a promotion, how much effort would it take to contact your prospects and customers to let them know? If you had an e-mail list, it could be done in minutes.

MARKETING MASTERY TIP #4

Embrace that technology is not going anywhere.

Exercise: Marketing Technology

Do you have a website? **Y / N**

Do you have at least 1 social media account? **Y / N**

Can clients purchase a product or service online from you? **Y / N**

MISTAKE #5
IGNORING THE PROBLEM, THINKING IT WILL RESOLVE ITSELF

"You cannot fix a problem that you refuse to acknowledge."

-Margaret Heffernan

The absolute WORST mistake that will cost you clients and cash is knowing that your marketing is failing but not being willing to devote the resources necessary to fix it.

You may know exactly what the problem is and you may have ideas on how to fix it, you're just too busy and overwhelmed to spend time on it.

Here's what typically happens, business owners will spend several hours "researching" aka asking friends and family, what they think about a marketing idea. Furthermore asking someone who has no marketing background what their opinion is about trying a "band-aid" method. Once they receive enough confirmed Yes from their inner circle, then they have the confidence to move forward and invest dollars into that marketing strategy. The problem is often more times than none the rate of return doesn't yield the results they had desired. Then the domino effect starts with cutting back on marketing budget, trying multiple strategies for too short of period, not leveraging technology...all of these leading to a downward spiraling business model.

As a business owner, your time is always too short and your to-do list is always too long. It's easy to push marketing issues to the bottom of the list when you have clients to serve. It's also like just turning the heater up during the winter instead of fixing the giant hole in the wall.

Your time is best spent serving your clients. Your clients chose you for your reputation and expertise. Taking time away from your clients to fix a marketing problem is rarely beneficial. Just as you know how to serve your clients well within your realm of expertise, a marketing expert knows how to design and implement a marketing plan that drives customers to your business.

CONCLUSION

Don't neglect marketing because it's too difficult, confusing or time consuming. Also don't assume that a general campaign will drive the clients you want. Failing to avoid these 5 mistakes outlined in this book provides ample opportunity for your competitors to steal your business.

Remember marketing is all about creating awareness that you exist. If someone that needs your services doesn't know you exist, they cannot consider you as an option to buy from.

I strongly recommend taking a few minutes to go back and answer the exercise questions under the each of the marketing mastery tips. If you need some further clarity on any of the marketing topics, or if you would like to schedule a time for a FREE initial consultation to discuss your business goals, email info@24hrprinter.com with the subject line "Marketing Help".

ABOUT THE AUTHOR

Leading strategist on merging corporate and entertainment entities, **Derrick Banes** is the brainchild of iBrand Consulting and founder of **24hrprinter.com**. After attending the University of North Texas, he worked with an array of Fortune 500 companies—from Adidas to Arista Records—with a tenacious work ethic and profound passion to help businesses thrive. Driven and always expanding his knowledge, Banes has gained a wide range of wisdom from industry giants and continues to learn from the best of the best. An expert in building brands, cross-promoting, and staying relevant, he's an out-of-the-box marketing strategist dedicated to promoting unrestricted creative and artistic expression in the business realm. Always a forerunner with a boundless thirst for discovering and innovating, Derrick Banes is a pioneering marketing expert with much to offer. Whether a business is in need of a great foundation or a fresh start, he is enthusiastic about coming alongside others in their professional ventures and helping them find the success they've long desired.

To receive **FREE** marketing tips, marketing product reviews, and monthly product discounts, visit **www.24hrprinter.com** and subscribe to our email list!